GW00375322

Contents

Mortar Peices put
upon the Tower

BEAU BRUMMEL
S-287181
43
RSY 474V

Mortars on the roof of the White Tower. A 17th-century playing card. British Museum

Arsenal to Museum

Fort Nelson, built for a war that never came, once the windswept home to a few soldiers and their families, now houses the Royal Armouries' extraordinary collection of artillery. This arsenal originated at the medieval heart of English military strength – the Tower of London. The Tower, as well as chief royal castle, mint and prison, was the administrative centre for the supply of arms and armour, including artillery, to the army and navy until 1855. As early as 1400, the Tower had become the main storehouse of artillery in England and a centre of production. But it was King Henry VIII who made the Tower famous for its great train of artillery. Artillery was both powerful symbol and actual part of a country's armed strength. At the time of Henry's death the Tower contained 64 bronze and 350 iron guns of all sizes. We know this because it was usual for a list, called an inventory, to be made of all possessions on the death of the monarch. The one made after the death of King Henry VIII in 1547 gives a wonderful insight into the belongings of this larger-than-life figure. Many of the guns listed had been imported because the young Henry intended to play power politics in Europe. English foundries were not geared up then for the massive re-armament that Henry demanded. But one imported gun never made it into the inventory: it was lost in transit in Dover Harbour from where it was recovered by chance in 1914. Henry imported craftsmen as well as guns: members of the Italian Arcana family were brought to work in England. Foreign craftsmen shook up the home industry: the Owen brothers were soon casting guns to rival Continental products. Guns were among the most expensive and useful presents between friendly rulers. Mons Meg, the great wrought-iron bombard on the books of the Royal Armouries but kept at its historic home, Edinburgh Castle, was presented by Philip the Good of Burgundy to King James II of Scotland. During the 18th century, the Tower was succeeded by the Royal Arsenal at Woolwich as the country's major artillery depot. The Tower became increasingly a showplace, overloaded with historic ordnance. Trophies of war provided additional guns, but one of the most splendid pieces

Previously at Eridge in Kent, from 1784 this English wrought-iron bombard was outside Boxted Hall, Suffolk. It was acquired from there by the Royal Armouries in 1979. The bombard was built about 1450 to fire stone balls and its construction of strips of iron bound by bands or hoops can clearly be seen. XIX.314

After the 1841 fire in the Tower of London: *View of the ruins of the Grand Storehouse.* Detail from a lithograph by Francis Ireland, after a drawing by Edward Falkener. I.358

in the collection, the great Turkish bombard of 1464, was presented by Turkey to Queen Victoria in 1868. This can be seen in the Artillery Hall near to sections of the infamous Iraqi Supergun. It is intriguing to find that both of these monster guns made over 500 years apart are smoothbores, that is, they are not rifled, and both are made in sections. In the case of the Supergun its total length would have been 156 metres.

The collection is constantly growing with the addition of rare pieces that show how artillery developed its potential. It is worth looking out for any or all of the following pieces. Another monster, the Victorian 38-ton rifled muzzle-loading gun of 12.5-inch calibre dated 1872 came from a coast defence battery on the Isle of Wight. The wrought-iron Boxted Bombard of about 1450 would have been used for attacking castle or town walls. More modern equipment, such as the impressive anti-aircraft guns of World War II, the menacing anti-tank weapons and the Sexton self-propelled 25-pounder are to be found in the Artillery Hall. The tradition of trophy guns has been maintained with two captured Iraqi guns from the Gulf War.

Positioning the 12.5-inch Rifled Muzzle-Loading gun (RML) of 38 tons on the Parade. The gun was once mounted at Cliff End Battery on the Isle of Wight. XIX.862

Long before many of these acquisitions were made, it had been realized that the Tower of London was quite unable to display a representative collection of artillery properly. The Royal Armouries was fortunate to discover Fort Nelson, which had been bought for preservation by Hampshire County Council. After careful restoration by Hampshire, the greater part of the collection was installed in galleries showing the development and manufacture of artillery. Guns mounted in the correct emplacements in the fort, regular firing demonstrations and live interpretations help truly bring Fort Nelson back to life and provide an exciting educational and enjoyable experience for visitors of all ages.

A quiet corner of the Fort. The English cast-iron Rose & Crown gun dates from about 1700. It is mounted on a replica field carriage. XIX.321

The main entrance to Fort Nelson. The bridge was originally a kind of drawbridge designed by Mr T C Guthrie before 1870. Instead of being pulled up, it was dragged into the fort supported by massive pivoting struts below.

Elevation and depression of a field gun. From *Archiley Kriegskunst*, by Johann Jacobi von Wallhausen, 1617.

WHAT IS ARTILLERY?

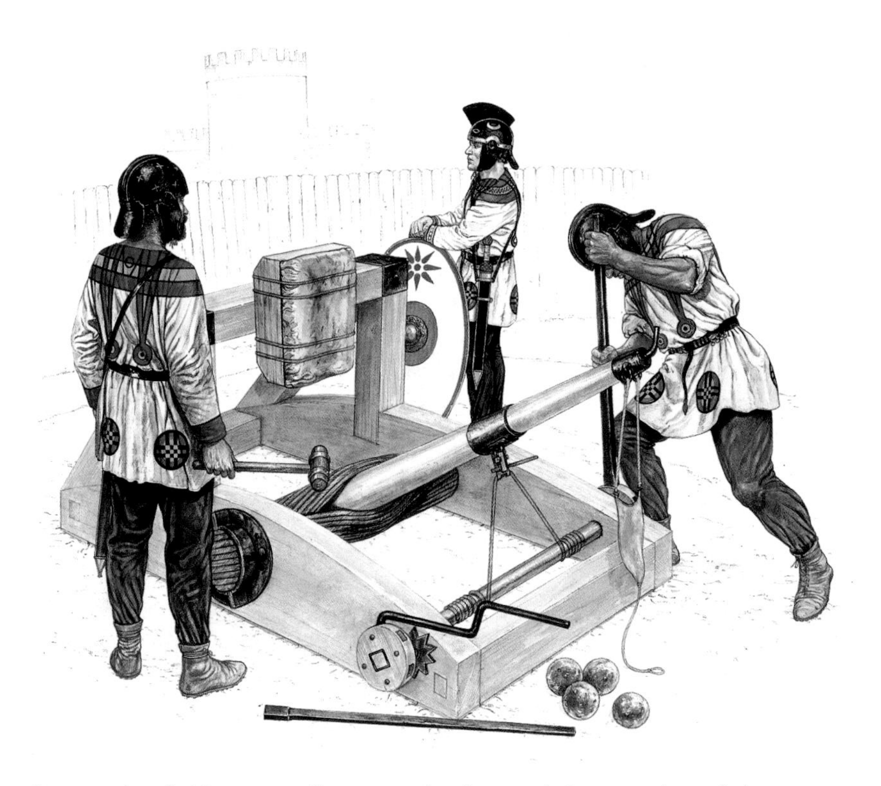

Reconstruction of a 4th-century AD Roman stone-throwing catapult. It was sometimes called an *onager*, the Latin word for a mule, presumably because it kicked like one. Illustration by Jeffrey Burn

Artillery provides a means of fighting at a distance. It is not restricted to gunpowder weapons. Slings and bows and ingenious medieval siege machines were called artillery and had the same purpose – that is, to do as much damage as possible from a range beyond hand-to-hand fighting. Siege warfare showed how dangerous close-range fighting could be, as Uriah the Hittite found when King David wanted to get him out of the way and sent him to his death at the siege of Rabbah. Even a stone thrown by hand is a form of artillery and one much used in siege and street fighting. It is the stone – or whatever projectile is cast at the enemy – that does the damage. One line of artillery development uses a projectile which itself contains the means of propulsion – the rocket. It is possible that the rocket was invented in China before what is known as tube artillery. At the Royal Armouries, Fort Nelson, artillery is taken to exclude rockets and hand-held weapons and deals mainly with the history of 'cannon' or simply 'guns', as they will usually be called here. There was a long history of ingenious mechanical artillery weapons before gunpowder was discovered. The replacement of mechanical siege engines by gunpowder artillery by the 15th century suggests that, not too long after the first illustration of a gun in 1326, gunpowder had the edge over the old artillery.

Piece of armour from a Sherman tank of about 1942. This has been used later as a target showing attack by British 6-pounder Anti-Tank (AT) shot. XXIII.69

Flat Trajectory Firing

A gunner is inserting the powder ladle into the gun. Then the shot (cannon ball) will be loaded. This had to be a loose fit to avoid jamming but the gap between the shot and bore allowed much of the force of the gunpowder to escape.

While one gunner is showing the sighting device to another, the gun is being aimed by a third. This shows how the taper of the barrel is allowed for by the device to give a line of sight parallel to the bore of the gun; this process is called disparting.

The gun is discharged by the gunner applying his portfire to the vent. The gun is laid 'point blank' which means that the barrel is horizontal. The shot will follow a nearly horizontal trajectory for some 100–200 yards.

From a textbook on artillery and fortification by Allain Manesson Mallet called *Les Travaux de Mars,* 1672.

The challenge facing early gunmakers was to construct a container that would withstand the force generated by the weak powder of the time and direct it so as to propel the projectile, initially an arrow then often a stone ball, in the right direction. Many early guns had a very small chamber for the powder and a short, wide barrel to hold and give some direction to the shot. The force of the explosion of the charge acts outwards equally in all directions. The barrel is a pressure vessel that resists these forces in all but one direction. That direction is the muzzle from which the shot emerges. Within limits, it will go faster and therefore hit harder the more gunpowder is used in the chamber. However, gunmakers found difficulty in coping with the increased pressures resulting from larger charges or improved powder. It appears that some kind of safety was achieved by using very loose-fitting shot or cannon balls which allowed a lot of the force to escape harmlessly.

Right: High-angle fire from siege mortars throwing bombs against a fortified town. On the left a gunner is carrying out the dangerous operation of lighting the time fuze before firing the main charge. *Les Travaux de Mars,* 1672.

Above: The first large shot were laboriously carved from blocks of stone – granite, marble and hard limestone were all used as available. Stone shot remained in use for many years. There were still 40 'stone shott ready hewed' (carved) in the 'Tower at Portsmouth' in 1550. Illustration by Jeffrey Burn

THE FIRST GREAT GUNS

Right: A 15th-century wrought-iron bombard similar to the Boxted bombard on show. Loading could not be hurried and at the short effective range of the bombard, the crew were vulnerable to enemy fire from firearms and bow-shot. The bombard and its crew, therefore, were protected by the pivoting timber shield. Illustration by Jeffrey Burn

The armoured knight on horseback, the longbow and crossbow and the high castle did not fall immediately to early gunpowder weapons. Perhaps by the early 15th century artillery had become a real force in warfare. Certainly, the capture of Constantinople by the Turks in 1453 proved that the fate of empires could be settled by big guns. None survives from that siege but the great Turkish bombard in the Artillery Hall was cast not long after, in 1464. Like the massive forged iron bombards of Northern Europe, it was designed to fire large stone balls. It must have been found that stone projectiles had to be very heavy in order to have any effect on strong medieval masonry. Even so, the range had to be short because neither the strength of the gun or the powder was up to producing high velocity of shot. Bombards were heavy siege pieces, difficult to move and needing their own local defence against the small arms and raids of the besieged. A notable feature of this Turkish bombard is that it was cast in two parts and screwed together. Probably the chief reason for casting the gun in two sections was because of its sheer size. Just to get the mass of bronze melted was an undertaking taking several days and phenomenal amounts of fuel. Having decided to make this gun in two sections,

Below: Model of Mons Meg, the great wrought-iron bombard made at Mons in the Low Countries in 1449. Made by Jean Cambier to the order of Duke Philip the Good of Burgundy (1396–1467) the gun was presented to King James II of Scotland in 1457. Mons Meg was removed from Edinburgh Castle in 1754 and displayed at the Tower of London until 1829. In 1835, back in Edinburgh Castle, its carriage collapsed. A new ornate cast-iron carriage was made for it at the Royal Arsenal, Woolwich in 1836 and it is believed that this model was made first to show how it would look. The full-size iron carriage was scrapped in 1934 when replaced by an historically more accurate timber carriage. This model appears to have been damaged in the Tower fire of 1841. XIX.148

GREAT TURKISH BOMBARD – THE DARDANELLES GUN

This is a famous example of the heavy artillery adopted so effectively by the Ottoman Turks. It was cast in 1464 for Sultan Mehmet II (1430–81) who had used heavy artillery to breach the massive defensive walls of Constantinople in 1453, marking the fall of the Christian Byzantine Empire. None of the artillery of this great siege is known to survive but this bombard is thought to be similar to those siege weapons. This bombard, however, is unusual in being made in two parts. It is a triumph of medieval technology, introduced to Turkey from the West. The barrel is threaded to accept the projecting screw thread of the breech or chamber. You can see the sockets for stout levers used to screw and unscrew the two massive components. Making this 20-ton bombard in two sections might have been in order to make the casting process easier – the amount of bronze (an alloy of copper and tin) that had to be melted for each half was still prodigious. Another advantage might have been that the enormous powder charge would be easier to load if the barrel were unscrewed from the chamber for each shot. The stone ball, weighing about 304 kg would be loaded into the barrel separately; a high rate of fire was not expected – perhaps 15 rounds per day.

This great bombard is sometimes known as the Dardanelles gun because later in its long service career it was mounted with other huge bronze guns to command the Dardanelles straits. Indeed, they were still being fired early in the 19th century when improved carriages were provided for them.

This picture shows the gun when it was still kept outdoors; it has been moved under cover to ensure its preservation as one of the most important artillery pieces to survive from the Middle Ages.

It was acquired from the Turkish government in 1868 and was formerly on show at HM Tower of London. XIX.164

a chamber for the powder and a barrel, the question remains open: was it a very early breech-loader, unscrewed for loading each round? This would have made cleaning and loading easier. But a lot of time and labour would have been taken in manipulating the heavy breech and barrel.

Breech-loaders were to have a prominent place in warfare, in the form both of bronze and of wrought-iron guns, for over a century. Recent trials by the Royal Armouries and the Mary Rose Trust have shown that the wrought-iron breech-loading port piece was capable of piercing a ship's side at close range. In the case of light swivel guns, the convenience of breech-loading ensured their use well into the 17th century. Heavy calibre breech-loaders were not to reappear until the middle of the 19th century.

Engraving of the Turkish Fort of Chanak showing several large pieces of ordnance. From a sketch by Lieutenant M O'Reilly reproduced in *Illustrated London News*, 15 July 1854.

Above: This cast-iron gun bears the arms of the Commonwealth, combining the English cross of St George with the Irish harp. They replaced the Royal Arms between 1649 and 1660, when Britain was a republic. Very few Commonwealth guns exist – or can be recognized – today because any found with these arms at the Restoration of King Charles II had them chiselled off – by order. This gun survived because it was lost at sea. It was trawled up by a Dutch fisherman in 1984 on the site of the battle of Scheveningen, fought on 31 July 1653, when the English fleet soundly beat the Dutch. XIX.325

Artillery on Land and Sea

King Charles VII of France caused a sensation when he invaded Italy in 1494, using powerful yet movable guns. A combination of technological improvements created this new artillery, such as improved powder propelling, the use of cast-iron instead of stone balls and strong bronze tubes loaded at the muzzle. Muzzle-loading had its disadvantages; but there must have been a worthwhile trade-off in obtaining a single piece barrel not weakened by a breech mechanism. In any case, the new guns prompted a fresh approach to fortification and gave the West an enormous advantage in armed ocean-going ships. These were crucial to the creation of trading posts in the East. Despite the obvious disadvantages of muzzle-loading at sea, gradually the bronze muzzle-loader began to replace wrought-iron breech-loaders as main armament. For example, the *Mary Rose* which sank in 1545 was armed with both.

Bronze guns were cast in a confusing variety of sizes, and some were built to fire stone shot like the old bombards. The chief disadvantage of the bronze gun whatever its picturesque name, from *basilisk* to *falconet*, was that bronze was an expensive material. Cast iron was more difficult to make and was not as strong as bronze. But when the founders of the Weald of England discovered how to make reliable cast-iron guns during the 16th century, a much cheaper form of artillery became available. Bronze was preferred for field guns, and at least partly for appearance' sake on first-rate ships, for many years. Jean Maritz improved the manufacture of bronze guns by casting them solid and then machining out the bore, a method quickly adopted by most gunfounders. It was more difficult to bore cast-iron guns in this way but John Wilkinson succeeded in England by 1774. But until the introduction of industrial quantities of wrought iron and steel in the 19th century, there was little significant change for 400 years. The mobility of guns on land remained a challenge; light guns to keep up with cavalry were introduced in the 18th century by most powers following the Prussian example.

That century also saw the application of a more logical approach to gun design. This was led by Jean-Baptiste Gribeauval, on whose complete system most of Europe and the USA as well as his native France based their artillery. In Britain, Benjamin Robins published an advanced theory of ballistics in 1742 which became the subject of extensive trials at Woolwich. Unfortunately, their findings were not applied directly to artillery in service. The 18th century saw greater understanding of ballistics and manufacturing techniques; the practical results were not to be seen until the mid 19th century.

Left: Two French three-barrelled bronze guns captured at the battle of Ramillies, 1706. King Louis XIV of France had a healthy respect for the firepower of the English under their commander, the Duke of Marlborough. It is tempting to think that the French three-barrelled guns, kept secret until the last minute, were intended to redress the balance during the War of Spanish Succession in which the power of France was curbed. XIX.51, 52

Nevertheless, ballistics theory aside, artillery in the hands of great commanders was still a battle-winning arm. But mobility of field artillery remained a problem. Frederick the Great of Prussia had shown the way forward by forming the first battery of horse artillery in 1759 – Britain and France followed. The Royal Horse Artillery, intended to act with cavalry, was formed in 1793. Unfortunately the 'Drivers', responsible for bringing the guns into action, were not always reliable. During the Peninsular campaign when the British were fighting the French with Portuguese and Spanish help, the British drivers were described by an artillery officer as a 'nest of infamy.' At Waterloo the guns, including those of the Horse Artillery, were used mainly defensively. While contributing to victory, the gunners were worn out by continually running up the guns after recoil. They did not use the horses, certain that they would be shot by the enemy. Under Napoleon, Corsican artillery officer turned Emperor, massed artillery had become decisive on the battlefields of Europe.

French 12-pounder field gun of Gribeauval type manned by a crew of Napoleon's Garde Imperiale of the time of Waterloo (1815).
Illustration by Jeffrey Burn

The Channel and the Royal Navy were Britain's only defence during much of the Napoleonic Wars. Timber line-of-battle ships mounted heavy broadside guns, around 40 or more per side, that with good drill and at short range could prove devastating. Traditionally, the French tried longer-range gunnery while the British waited until the range was very short – perhaps about fifty to a hundred yards – giving great effect to the guns, which were often double shotted. This was seen at Trafalgar, when HMS *Victory* had to accept casualties from long range enemy fire before she could close for action. When she did, raking the stern of the *Bucentaure,* the *Victory* caused enormous damage. It would take nearly half a century for gunnery ranges to lengthen.

One of the many pieces from Ranjit Singh's impressive artillery train captured during the Sikh Wars in the 1840s, this field gun is complete with its original carriage and limber. The decorated carriage with its prominent display of a favourite Indian technique – hard-wood inlaid with brass – does not impair the efficiency of the piece based closely on the Congreve pattern introduced in British service during the late 18th century. This gun was acquired by the Royal Armouries from the family of Sir Hugh, later Viscount, Gough, commander of the British forces that defeated the Sikhs. XIX.329

The crowned initials of the reigning monarch can be seen cast or engraved on British gun barrels. While this device, known as a cipher, could be a decorative feature, its main purpose was to show that the gun belonged to the British Crown. This is the cipher of Queen Victoria (1837–1901). Another version can be seen carved into the stone work at the main entrance to Fort Nelson.

Artillery, Industry and the Arms Race

The specially built 'Armstrong' factory, part of the Royal Gun Factory in the Royal Arsenal. After the breech-loading guns designed by Sir William Armstrong proved unreliable, rifled muzzle-loading (RML) guns were built on similar principles. Here new heavy RML guns are being placed outside the factory, conveniently near the Thames.

Until Victorian engineers approached the subject from first principles, guns were merely tubes cast without detailed knowledge of the behaviour and ideal structure of pressure vessels. Among the almost forgotten innovators were the Irish engineers Robert Mallet and Alexander Blakely who were quick to see the necessity of built-up construction for guns. This had been realized in America by Daniel Treadwell. He understood that to make a gun barrel stronger it had to be built up in layers, not just cast thicker. His ideas were adopted by Sir William (later Lord) Armstrong who introduced the first rifled artillery into British service in 1859. The mechanical strength of guns was only one worry: by the 1850s there were serious concerns over the weight of guns relative to their performance. Their lack of range in face of the new rifles in the hands of infantry threatened the traditional superiority of artillery. Many other inventors in Europe and America tried their hand at artillery design. Some of their names are still familiar today: Henry Bessemer whose famous process for bulk production of steel was inspired by his artillery experiments, and Sir Joseph Whitworth whose standardized thread-form still bears his name and whose accuracy of machining was phenomenal. Even the 16th-century technique of hoop-and-stave gun building was studied. By the 1880s large guns had appeared, representing the most potent engines of destruction until aircraft entered warfare. Built of high-grade steels,

Right: Rifled artillery was the great achievement of mid 19th-century pioneering gun designers. Long familiar for small arms, rifling was much harder to apply successfully to artillery. But it did result in the production of much more efficient and accurate guns with greater effective range. Rifling – spiral grooves cut into the barrel – spins the projectile as it is fired to stabilize it in flight.

they were rifled, breech-loading, had full recoil control and auxiliary powered mountings for laying on the target directed with the use of sophisticated instruments. In less than 50 years there had been an almost complete revolution in gunnery. Another decade would see smokeless powder and the ability to fit recoil control on to field gun carriages. The Industrial Revolution created a vast manufacturing industry in Great Britain, closely followed by other powers such as France, Germany and America. Previously undreamed-of capacity now existed for the mass production of large complicated fighting machines such as the battleship and artillery weapons of all sizes for land warfare. Railways could move armies and their equipment quickly over great distances. Technological developments were hard for governments to assess but resulted in enormous expenditure being committed to maintain the balance of power. The international arms trade encouraged competition between countries to build ever greater arsenals and persuaded even small countries which could ill afford the cost to buy modern arms. Despite her wealth Britain felt, with her vast empire, the heavy burden of the arms race. The First World War revealed what pitiless horrors were unleashed when heavily industrialized countries went to war.

Above: One of the first heavy guns produced in the early 1880s when Britain found herself obliged to return quickly to breech-loading artillery. This is a 12-inch gun weighing 43 tons. From a contemporary photograph. I.1245

Below: Competitive trials of different rifled guns at Shoeburyness in 1863. This was the period when the government was trying to assess the claims of rival designers in order to select the best system of rifling and whether breech-loading or muzzle-loading would be better for British service. As the ranges of guns increased with the introduction of rifling, a longer range had to be found than was available near the government arsenal at Woolwich. At Shoeburyness in Essex firing could take place over the marshes and shallow tidal water.

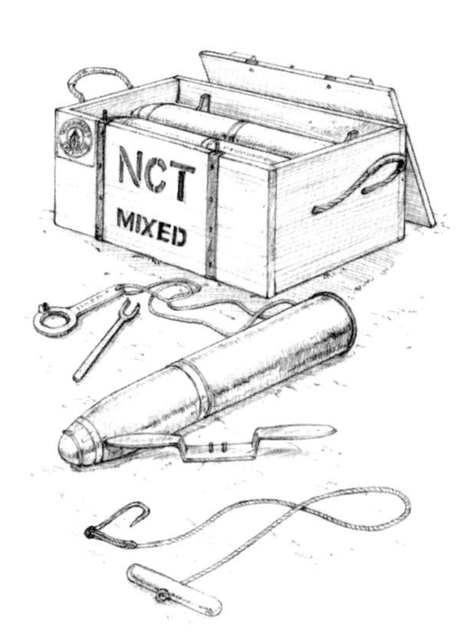

Above: 18-pounder QF ammunition was supplied in wooden boxes containing four rounds of 'fixed ammunition'. 'NCT' on the box refers to the nitrocellulose cartridge filling sometimes used during the First World War instead of cordite. A round is shown in front; the projectile is attached to the cartridge case containing the propellant so that it could be loaded very quickly. Nearby is a tool for fitting and removing primers. A firing lanyard and fuze keys are also visible. Illustration by Jeffrey Burn

Right: A British 18-pounder QF field gun in action during the First World War. One of the heaviest-hitting field guns when introduced in 1904, the 18-pounder fired nearly 100 million rounds during the stupendous barrages of the 1914–18 war. The 18-pounder remained in service in later versions until the late 1930s. There is an example dated 1917 (XIX.529) on show in the Artillery Hall with a replica limber which allows the gun to be used in special events when it is sometimes towed by horses. Courtesy the Imperial War Museum

The Red God of War

Artillery in the 20th century

Josef Stalin memorably called artillery the 'red god of war'. Although aircraft, missiles and atomic weapons were developed capable of global devastation, nevertheless in the 20th century artillery still won battles. Tanks are still armed with guns; some forces still use guns for anti-aircraft purposes and it has been found imprudent to remove naval guns from warships. The 19th century prepared all the main technology for 20th-century guns as machines, just as the basic principles of the motor car were in place before the First World War. But a modern gun does not look much like, say, the French 75 mm M1897, the most advanced field gun in service at the turn of the century and typical of the field guns of the First World War. Nor does a modern car look much like one of that period. But the changes have been in small steps – improved metals, lubricants, the use of plastics and the introduction of electronics, especially in computing and control mechanisms. On land, the replacement of horses by the internal combustion engine resulted in a complete change in the life of the gunner and the tactical mobility of artillery. Better design of ammunition aerodynamically and techniques such as rocket-assisted projectiles have made possible increases of range up to 40 km, for which Dr Gerald Bull, designer of the Supergun, was noted.

88 mm Flak 37. This example of the celebrated German Second World War Anti-Aircraft (AA) gun is dated 1944. The '88' was able to fire at ground targets as well and was used to devastating effect against British tanks in North Africa. The British eventually arranged for the 3.7-inch AA gun to be used in the same way. XIX.331

Fuze design relied on purely mechanical means until the miniaturization of electronic components allowed the production of proximity fuzes in which a tiny radio transmitter senses when the shell is near enough to the target to explode effectively. By the 1930s smaller calibres in which a rapid rate of fire is vital could be automatic. The principle was extended to heavier calibres. An alternative was a semi-automatic system like that of the British 6-pounder Anti–Tank gun where speed was of the essence. These have brass cartridge cases to contain the powder charge. Brass cartridge cases are also used with manually loaded field guns; this system is known as quick-firing or QF. Advantages are that the case serves to seal the breech of the gun on firing and is a robust item. The other system, loading with bagged charges, is known, somewhat confusingly as breech-loading or BL. Of course both are loaded at the breech. The difference is that BL guns need a mechanical device to seal the breech. They are generally heavier calibres and often have beautifully machined and complicated screw-thread breeches.

The high altitude research project (acronym HARP) gun in Barbados. This was used by Dr Gerald Bull to carry out experiments that led to the Supergun. Courtesy Dr Alan George

Armies soon got bogged down during the First World War. Howitzers like the British 6-inch howitzer and siege pieces including huge railway guns were used to try to break the deadlock. Tanks were also introduced. Between the First and Second World Wars experiments took place to fit guns to motorized chassis. Artillery could then provide fire support to fast-moving armoured forces. The British Sexton self-propelled gun introduced in 1944 made use of the 25-pounder gun/howitzer on a tank chassis to offer versatile mobile firepower. Tanks and aircraft challenged gun designers. High-velocity weapons were developed to provide the punch to attack armoured vehicles. For different reasons, high velocity – and sophisticated fire control and fuze technology – were required for anti-aircraft defence. The difficulty was in predicting where such a fast-moving target would be so that the shell could arrive close enough to the aircraft to destroy it. The Anti-Tank gun needed to be accurate and have enough penetrating power to defeat armour plate. At the outbreak of the Second World War Anti-Tank guns were small calibre weapons. They soon had to be replaced by increasingly heavy weapons. Even massive Anti-Aircraft guns such as the German '88' and British 3.7-inch were used against tanks.

One of two sections of the Iraqi Supergun on show at Fort Nelson after being intercepted by British Customs in 1990. There were more pieces of the same tube and one section of another, smaller gun, known as Baby Babylon also designed by the Canadian Dr Gerald Bull, in the same shipment. The chamber tube of the smaller gun is also on show in the Artillery Hall. XIX.842

Recoilless artillery and even hand-held weapons eventually replaced Anti-Tank guns, helped by the development of shaped charges to blow holes in armour rather than heavy, high-velocity projectiles designed to punch through it.

From the late 19th century mechanical computing helped with the calculations to direct a projectile on to the target. In the 21st century gun design continues with experimental electromagnetic weapons and liquid-propelled projectiles. The main 20th-century collection including the pieces mentioned in the text, is displayed in the Artillery Hall.

The Art of War

Guns as sculpture

Right: This ornate bronze 18-pounder can be found on the parade. A poem is inscribed on the gun, beginning by naming the sultan who ordered it: *That sun of sovereignty who cast his rays over East and West, namely Sultan Ahmed II, the ruler whose attendants are as numerous as the stars...* Turkish, dated 1708. XIX.115

Above: The end face of its trunnion is decorated with stylized flower patterns.

A dragon's head makes an appropriate ornate gun muzzle, breathing fire and destruction. The rest of this bronze gun is made to resemble the dragon's body. It was taken by British forces from King Thebaw's palace in Mandalay in 1885. Burmese, late 18th century. XIX.123

Bronze gave gun-founders and their powerful customers the ideal material for creating highly ornamental pieces of artillery. Decorated guns remained just as deadly as the plainer versions but it is clear that a few guns in the Royal Armouries collection must have been cast almost purely for show. The Italian gun and carriage for the Knights of St John, the dragon gun from Burma and the Indian tiger mortar are examples: the latter was never finished as a weapon and is made of very weak metal. Guns always represented a large investment; iron barrels gave little scope for decoration although the quality of the forging of details of the wrought-iron guns shows flourishes of honest workmanship. Cast-iron guns often had a simple raised royal cipher or badge such as the English 'Rose and Crown' guns with their royal badge based on their bronze Tudor prototypes. Even into the 20th century, steel guns had the British royal monogram neatly engraved on their barrels. But the cost of bronze guns and the fact that they were often made by founders who also cast sculpture resulted in decoration which would reveal to all how valuable they were. Nevertheless some of the plainest 16th-century guns are extremely fine and appeal to a particular kind of modern taste. A good example is the simple but beautifully proportioned octagonal gun for King Henri II of France. King Henry VIII's bronze guns varied from highly ornate to almost plain barrels of fine proportions with delicate decorative details. Many of the finest guns are shown in the Art Gallery along with paintings such as the early 17th-century *Venus at the Forge of Vulcan* attributed to Jan Breughel, and an early

Venus at the Forge of Vulcan, attributed to Jan Breughel (1601–78). The goddess Venus was married to the smith, Vulcan. Here she is shown visiting his forge. Despite the fanciful setting this early 17th-century painting shows much of the equipment that would have been found in an arsenal, including, beneath the arch on the left, machinery for cannon boring. I.38

18th-century English tapestry showing gun manufacture. But remember that it is possible to find guns with startling forms of decoration in other galleries and on the Parade. Strange creatures and intricate ornament sometimes appear at just the height for curious children to find. Occasionally, the carriage of a gun was also treated as a sculptural object or field at least for decorative treatment. The most striking example is the 17th-century carved wood carriage for the Knights of St John's gun, the trail of which consists of two 'Furies'. The Furies were ghastly female personifications of the spirits of death on the battlefield. The small gun presented about 1700 to Queen Anne's military enthusiast son, the young Duke of Gloucester, is still mounted on its original carriage. Few carriages of this date have survived; this one, while it follows the usual design of the time, is remarkable for its fine carved panels. Even the bill for the work exists. Henry Hayward, Master Carpenter to the Board of Ordnance, put in his detailed account for the work in 1699. It came to the then considerable sum of £45.

The lifting loops on gun barrels are commonly in the form of a stylized dolphin and are therefore often called dolphins. Here they are in the form of a heraldic beast known as a wyvern on a beautifully decorated Flemish gun of 1535. XIX.166

Bronze gun made for the Grand Master of the Knights of St John, Malta, known as the Furies gun. This is because the carriage is carved with female figures symbolizing death and destruction. The gun was cast in 1773 making use of an earlier design of 1684. Captured by the British from a French ship carrying booty from Malta in 1798. XIX.79

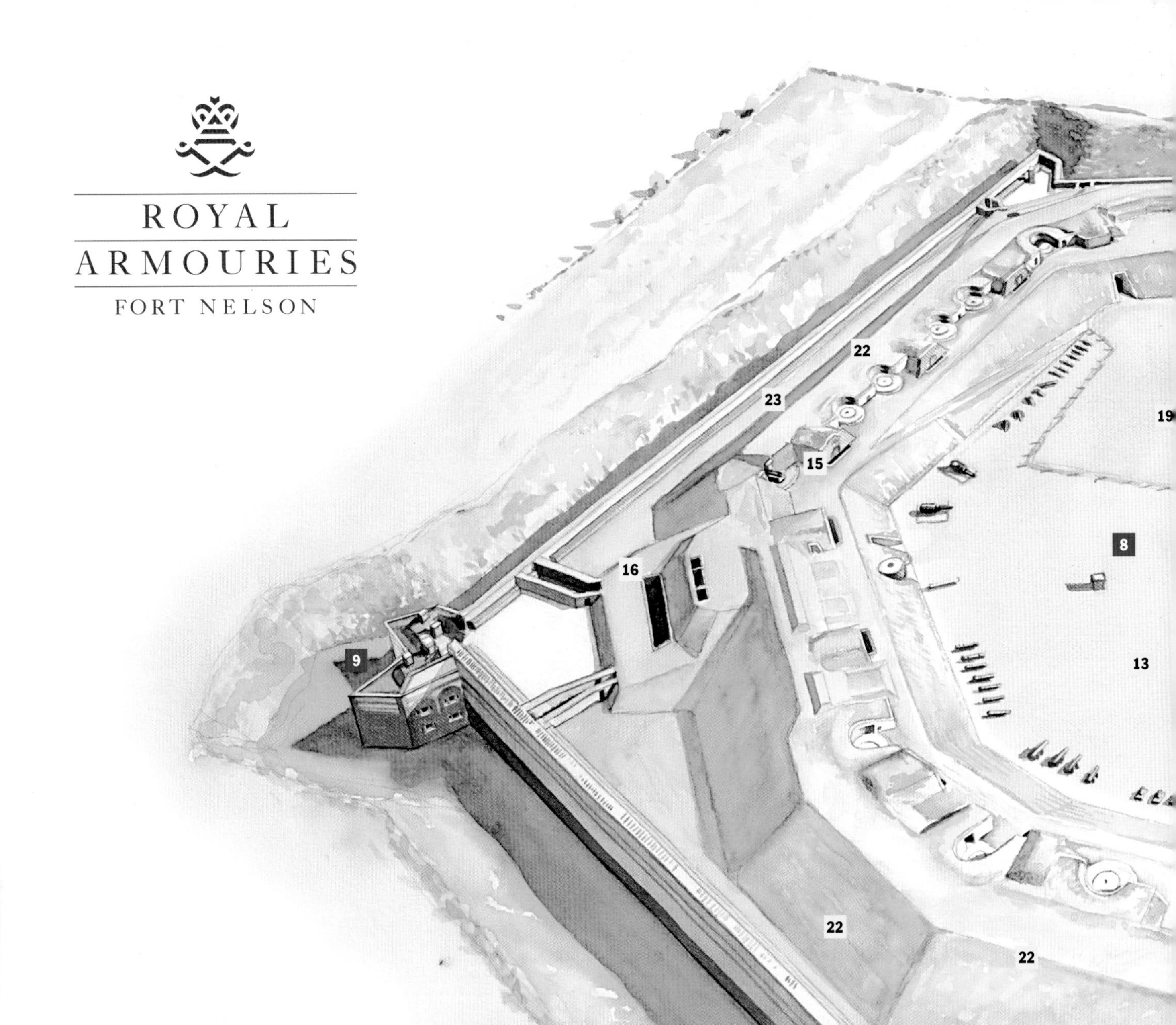

Fort Nelson Museum Guide

Lower Level & Tunnels

- 1 Main Entrance
- 2 Shop
- 3 Redan and Barracks
- 4 Powder Keg Cafe and Toilets
- 5 Galleries
- 6 Education & Resources Centre 2
- 7 Tunnel Entrance
- 8 Underground Magazines
- 9 North Caponier

Upper Level & Ramparts

- 10 West Haxo Casemate
- 11 West Demi Caponier
- 12 Artillery Hall
- 13 Parade
- 14 Dry Moat
- 15 Public View-Point
- 16 North Mortar Battery
- 17 West Mortar Battery
- 18 64-pounder Gun Emplacement
- 19 Daily Gun Salute Arena
- 20 Artillery Conservation Area
- 21 WWII Ammunition Sheds
- 22 Ramparts
- 23 68-pounder Gun Emplacement
- 24 Mallet's Mortar
- 25 14" Battleship Gun
- PD Parking for Disabled Persons
- P Museum Visitor Parking
- FD Functions/Corporate Car Park
- T Toilets
- TD Toilets for Disabled Persons

20
6
FP
4
T
3
24
P
12
7
21
21
5
1
TD
2
PD
25
18
10
14
14
11

Above: Detail of the initials or cipher of Queen Victoria as Victoria *Regina et Imperatrix* (queen and empress) carved in stone at the main entrance to Fort Nelson.

Right: Lord Palmerston (1784–1865) by Francis Cruickshank. Against a background of hostility and fear of France, Palmerston, supported by public opinion and Queen Victoria herself, adopted a strong defence policy. An important element was the fortifying of major ports as a result of the report of the 1860 Royal Commission.
By courtesy of the National Portrait Gallery

The Royal Commission of 1860

In the summer of 1860 fortification specialists of the Royal Engineers beat their way through standing wheat on peaceful Portsdown, making the best compensation deals they could with the tenants of the Southwick Estate. Their sense of urgency came from the highest level of Government. They were marking out on the ground the latest type of European fortification. A vast scheme of mutually supporting forts would girdle Portsmouth by land and sea. Soon the chalk hill would be gouged deeply to form dry moats and ramparts; in the case of Fort Widley excavations were sunk where the townsfolk had previously come to admire the view and take tea.

Fort Nelson was named for its neighbouring monument of 1807. This, the column and bust of Horatio, Lord Nelson, marked England's greatest naval victory at Trafalgar in 1805, the death of its greatest admiral and the beginning of a century of military anxieties. In Britain a period of alarm followed the Crimean War, fought against Russia by Britain and France as uneasy allies. France under Napoleon III was building up her military and naval strength. *Gloire*, the first of a new kind of armoured steam-powered warship, raised doubts as to Britain's ability to repel an invasion. These doubts caused Lord Palmerston to set up a Royal Commission to report on the defences of the United Kingdom with Portsmouth and its Royal Dockyard as the priority. Supported by Queen Victoria and her husband, Prince Albert, the result was the building of the greatest works of fortification yet undertaken in this country in peacetime. A start on modernizing the Royal Navy was made with the launch of HMS *Warrior*, the answer to *Gloire*, and Britain's traditional wooden walls began to be replaced with ironclads. The third element in strengthening Britain's defences was to augment the small standing army by the raising of new volunteer corps. Artillery volunteers were especially important and without them the extensive Portsmouth fortress could never have been garrisoned. Fort Nelson, along with the

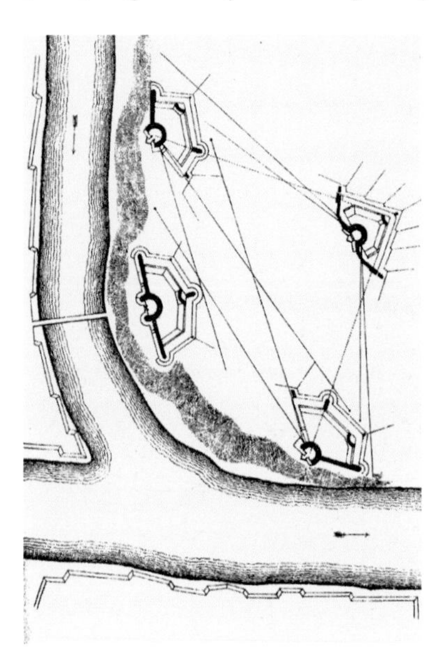

The so-called German or Prussian system of fortification formed the model for the Portsmouth defences. The main features were the separation of the long range and close defence armament, the simple polygonal plan – which gave rise to the alternative name *polygonal fortification* – and the siting of individual forts to protect each other by flanking fire. From the *Text Book of Fortification* Part II by Lieut-Col J F Lewis, 1893.

Map to show the location of the fortifications around Portsmouth.

other land works in this huge ring fortress around Portsmouth, was substantially complete by the late 1860s. The huge armament demands for the Royal Commission forts were never fully met. Fortunately the threat of invasion evaporated, so Fort Nelson and its neighbours were never put to the test. By the time they were nearly finished, France had been invaded and defeated by Prussia. Because the forts were not used to repel an invasion and perhaps because it seemed as though the forts pointed the wrong way – their guns aim inland – they soon became known locally as Palmerston's Folly. It could hardly be admitted officially that such was the pace of change both in technology and international relations, these forts were obsolete almost as soon as they were completed. They were therefore maintained and formed monumental props in the large-scale manoeuvres involving both regulars and volunteers during the later 19th century. The townsfolk with picnics, the tea-rooms having been demolished, flocked to watch the spectacle.

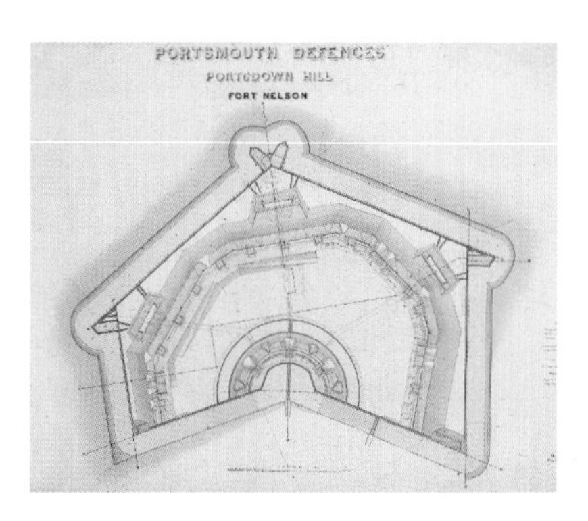

The polygonal shape of the Fort can be seen clearly in this early plan drawn by the Royal Engineers. It can be seen that the barracks building is semi-circular in plan, just like the earlier German forts shown opposite. However, when built, the design was changed to the triangular plan redan.
Public Record Office

An aerial view of Fort Nelson looking North. The pointed redan and barrack block behind can be seen in the foreground.

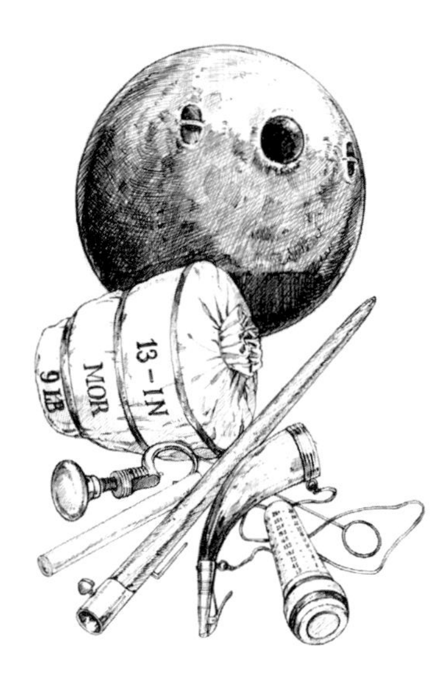

13-inch mortar ammunition. The cast-iron bomb was filled with gunpowder and fitted with a wooden time fuze that can be seen to the bottom right together with a priming flask and portfire and holder. The bagged gunpowder propellant charge or cartridge is shaped to fit the tapered chamber of the cast iron mortar. In front of the charge is a fuze-borer used to pierce the fuze to set its time of burning. At this period the fuze was no longer ignited separately by the gunner but was lit by the flame of the main charge passing through the gap between the bomb and the bore. Illustration by Jeffrey Burn

Deterring the Enemy
A massive artillery fortification

The Palmerston forts were built at a time of rapid change in artillery design. Fortification design had already undergone a fundamental change. The great 'bastioned' forts and city defences of the 17th and 18th centuries had become increasingly complicated in lay-out and impossible to arm and garrison properly. They were also astoundingly expensive. By the 1850s the latest Continental forts were based on the 'polygonal' system. This provided a much more compact fort with the ability, not available in the old bastioned system, of concentrating its main firepower on the besieger yet providing a wide field of fire. Close-range defence was provided by special gun positions covering the deep dry moat. If necessary the garrison could use rifles from the firing steps around the main *scarp* wall. The other innovation in the polygonal system was that, instead of enormously long continuous lines of fortification around an important town, a series of detached forts could defend each other by overlapping covering fire. Fort Nelson is part of such a chain around Portsmouth and its vital Royal Dockyard. Tunnels were included within the Fort so troops could get around the Fort under cover in action. The vital powder magazine was buried deep under the Parade. The earth-covered barracks, themselves defensible, were placed in the safest place away from the direction of enemy fire. At the same period weapon design was at last beginning to catch up with developments in civilian engineering resulting from the Industrial Revolution. The records for Fort Nelson reflect the transition from cast-iron smoothbore to built-up rifled guns. One is reminded of HMS *Warrior* launched in 1860, moored not far away in Portsmouth, also armed with both 68-pounder smoothbores and 110-pounder Armstrong guns. Originally, the intended main armament of Fort Nelson was entirely of cast-iron and smoothbore weapons: 68-pounders on the gun platform, 13-inch mortars in three concealed vaulted batteries and lighter guns for

68-pounder cast-iron gun dated 1847. Weighing nearly 5 tons (the official designation was 'of 95 cwt') this was one of the last of the massive smoothbore guns mainly intended for service with the Royal Navy. It could fire either a 68-pound solid shot or 8-inch spherical shell and was superseded by the 7-inch RBL gun. This 68-pounder is mounted on a replica garrison carriage in a restored embrasure and represents the originally intended main armament of the Fort. AL.182.1

64-pounder RML gun dated 1873. Converted from a cast-iron smoothbore 32-pounder, this type of gun was issued to forts in large numbers. It is mounted on a replica 'blocked up' carriage to fire over a high parapet. This helped protect the crew in action but complicated the gun drill. This can be seen when, on special days, the Portsdown Artillery Volunteers fire this gun. XIX.253

flank defence, mounted in *caponiers* and barracks. Examples are shown mounted in original emplacements. One 68-pounder on a replica carriage, six of the intended nine cast-iron 13-inch mortars, and one 32-pounder on an original carriage, defending the Redan represent the many flank pieces. Although the supply of guns was never sufficient to arm fully all the fixed fortifications of this country, great efforts were made to mount a significant proportion of the armament of key forts, and to do so at minimum cost to the Treasury. This gave rise to some unusual solutions. The present armament at Fort Nelson is based on that recorded in 1893 and covering the period until the fort was disarmed early in the 20th century. To show this period, there is a light 110-pounder (7-inch) Armstrong RBL gun in the West 'Haxo casemate'. Called after Napoleon Bonaparte's Engineer General, F B Haxo, who originally came up with this arrangement, the casemate is constructed on top of the gun platform to protect the gun and detachment from enemy fire. This Armstrong gun, probably the only surviving example of this light, 72-cwt type, was built at the Royal Gun Factory, Woolwich in 1862. Originally intended for the Royal Navy, these guns proved unpopular at sea on account of their violent recoil. They were consequently issued to forts to fire reduced charges. This one was acquired as an excavated barrel, lacking any fittings. To enable it to be interpreted properly, the Royal Armouries had a replica breech mechanism and replica mounting made to bring the gun into firing condition. Another piece mounted on the gun platform illustrates a much-used improvised type of fortress armament. It is a 64-pounder *Palliser* Rifled Muzzle-Loading gun, converted from a 32-pounder cast-iron smooth-bore. Captain Palliser's system used a combination of new scientific wrought-iron construction technology with the large supply of obsolete guns. A rifled wrought-iron tube was inserted in a suitably re-bored old cast-iron gun to make a more effective weapon that could still use its old mounting.

Above: 7-inch RBL Armstrong gun built at the Royal Gun Factory, Woolwich, in 1862; it has been restored to fire blank and is mounted on a replica carriage. XIX.506

Left: The cast-iron 13-inch mortar was near the end of its service life when Fort Nelson was prepared to receive nine of them in three protected batteries. Cumbersome to serve, the 13-inch mortar was nevertheless capable of throwing a heavy explosive bomb to about 3,000 yards with surprising accuracy. One of the Fort's 13-inch mortars is seen here being blank-fired by members of the Portsdown Artillery Volunteers. XIX.332

Above: Decorative air brick.

Right: A typical barrack room scene from an old photograph. This is not of Fort Nelson – it is clearly a hutted camp such as Aldershot, but shows the same furniture and atmosphere of a Victorian barracks.

The Garrison

'Usual occupation: I (Heavy) Battery Royal Garrison Artillery. Field Officers: 1. Officers: 5. Married Soldiers: 7. Sergeants: 4. Rank & File: 129. Horses, Officers': 9. Troop: 26.'

This bald official statement from early in the 20th century shows how the original intentions for Fort Nelson changed. After 1902 the fixed armament was removed and a battery of Royal Garrison Artillery was installed. In the 1901 Census there had been only one soldier, probably a NCO and 14 civilians: four male and ten female. In the 1911 Census there were 112 officers and men stationed at Fort Nelson. In fact, the Fort had become redundant against French aggression before it was quite finished in 1871. While the railway contractor Thomas Treadwell's men were completing the barracks and redan, France was suffering defeat by a vigorous Prussia, intent on leading German reunification. When Fort Nelson and the other Palmerston forts around Portsmouth were planned, the intention was to garrison them with volunteers. The British army was not large by European standards and was spread widely in answer to the demands of Empire. Joining the army, except as an officer, was not usually seen as a desirable option but rather an indication of escape from extreme poverty or some past misdemeanour. Conscription was a political impossibility. So, 'peaceable Victorians put on the dashing uniforms of a new volunteer movement.' The Volunteer movement, sanctioned in 1859, was immensely popular at least for the first few years and recruitment was enthusiastic.

The garrison of Fort Nelson had to learn gun drill and maintain a variety of armament. Here the crew of the 7-inch RBL Armstrong gun is represented. The gun is in the 'run-out' position and they are loading the projectile. Housed in the West Haxo casemate the special mounting consists of the carriage, which recoils up the platform. This is pivoted to traverse for quick aiming. Illustration by Jeffrey Burn

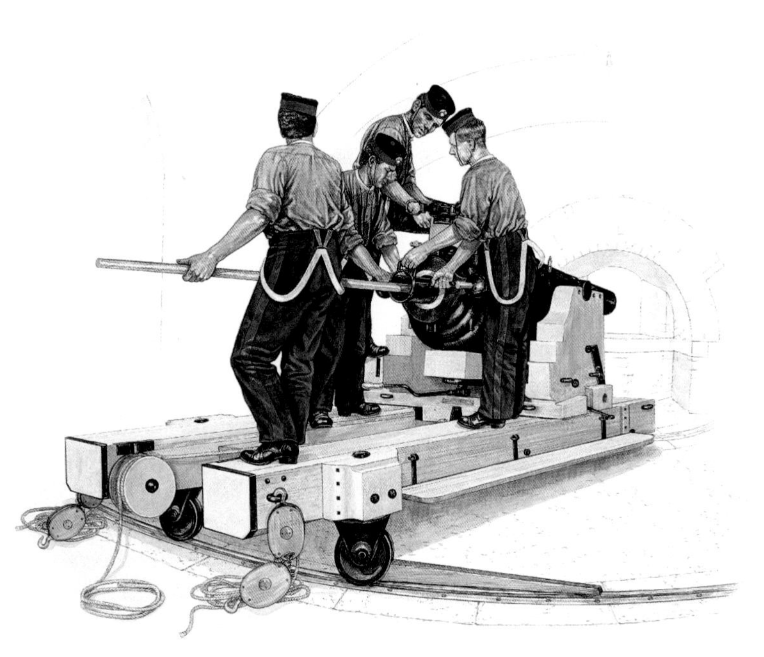

Artillery volunteers were based at the Palmerston forts where training and annual exercises were held to improve both gunnery and rifle shooting. In 1877 the 1st Hampshire Artillery Volunteers won the Queen's Prize at the National Artillery Association competition at the school of gunnery at Shoeburyness.

What were the garrison's living conditions like at Fort Nelson? By the 1870s army reforms had ensured that adequate, if basic, food was supplied. For the ranks meat and vegetables were simply boiled. More varied fare was prepared for officers and their guests in the more elaborate facilities of the officers' mess kitchen which has been restored.

Although a soldier's pay was low, it was not subject to so many deductions as before. For example the cost of food and drink was formerly taken out of the pay. Whatever pay money was left over might all too often be spent on drink. Discipline was strict, but alcohol was consumed in the 'wet canteen' near the main entrance. Any miscreants would be locked up in one of the cells behind the guard room. Tragically, a musketry instructor, Sergeant Carter, committed suicide here on 26 December 1875 after being reprimanded by the Commanding Officer, Captain Thomas Rose for being drunk on Christmas day.

Education – there was a schoolroom above the barracks – and other possibilities for sober improvement and entertainment were provided on site as welfare gradually was taken more seriously. A recreation room was constructed on the Parade where newspapers and books could be found.

The men slept twenty to each of the large barrack rooms; one of the smaller rooms has been restored. Each had a small open fire that must have been more for show than actual warmth. Not only were handsome sash windows fitted but also permanent internal ventilation was provided by special shafts and ducts. Many of the decorative air bricks and iron baffles can be seen. Even the fireplaces were supplied direct with fresh air from outside. Behind they had a simple heat exchanger to send warmed air into the room through a grating above head height. Stuffiness was ruthlessly prevented. Improvements in welfare resulted from Florence Nightingale's efforts during the Crimean War (1854–6) during which sickness took a terrible toll of the troops. Originally, hospital accommodation was provided at Fort Nelson – the Palmerston forts were seen as self-sufficient forts in the case of war.

Top: 'Wet Canteen': members of the garrison welcome visiting families at a fort. Illustration from a print of the mid 19th century

Above: The officers' mess kitchen complete with working cooking range.

Washing facilities, the 'ablutions' for NCOs and other ranks, are a shock to modern ideas of comfort. A small ablutions room can be seen near the main tunnel entrance. Iron bowls were used on slate slabs with piped cold water only. In addition there was a small bathroom with three baths, one being reserved for NCOs. Plenty of latrines were constructed. Open to the skies there can have been little incentive to loiter, especially in winter.

Some of the Victorian accommodation was used as late as the Second World War. However, the Commanding Officer was given a brand new bungalow. It was built along with the first of the Anti-Aircraft ammunition magazines on the Parade just before the outbreak of war in 1939.

This watercolour of Royal Garrison Artillery with a coast defence gun is dated 1910. It is by the well-known military artist Richard Simkin (1850–1926). Although it does not depict Fort Nelson, indeed the battery location is not recorded, it is interesting in showing gun crew dressed in the then new 1908 khaki uniform. In the foreground, the officers and men are in full dress, based on the late Victorian uniform of the Royal Artillery. I.1289

Above: The main tunnel gives access under cover from enemy fire to vital parts of the Fort. These are: the main magazines holding ammunition for the Fort's armament; the shaft and hoist for delivering ammunition to the guns; the North caponier and the North mortar battery. To the left can be seen the conveyor belt installed to handle Anti-Aircraft ammunition during the Second World War.

Right: The site of the Second World War Fort Nelson Anti-Aircraft battery today, from the air. It is not open to the public.

Fort Nelson

Adapted for 20th-century military use

Fort Nelson was disarmed early in the 20th century. This was part of the much-needed modernization of both Navy and Army that closed bases and swept away vast quantities of obsolete armament of an almost incredible variety of calibres and types. It was during the first half of the 20th century, though, that the Fort saw its busiest period ever. First, as a transit camp during the First World War and, second, during the Second World War, as an important Anti-Aircraft (AA) magazine and adjoining Anti-Aircraft battery. There are few signs of First World War alterations, but one interesting modification dating from the early years of the 20th century can be seen in the West Haxo casemate. Next to the emplacement containing the restored 110-pounder Armstrong gun, the southern casemate or arch can be seen partitioned off. When the guns were removed this was converted into a blacksmith's forge for the fort. This included farriery(shoeing horses) as there were then stables on the Parade. The forge has been restored to working order.

It was realized well before the Second World War that anti-aircraft defence would be crucial if Britain had to go to war. Fort Nelson was a vital part of the system of 'Air Defence Great Britain' as one of the major ammunition depots on the South Coast and one of the important batteries preventing enemy aircraft flying inland from the Channel. Starting in 1938, ten long brick and concrete magazines were built (two remain), covering the Parade, while even the Victorian underground magazine was adapted to hold Bofors 40 mm Anti-Aircraft ammunition. Steel lightning-conductor masts were erected on the barracks and ramparts, slit trenches were dug for local defence and crude bombs – glass bottles containing an incendiary mixture mainly for throwing by hand like a Molotov cocktail – were issued. Parts of the ramparts were cut away to allow lorries to circulate and the moat was filled in at the East drawbridge. A new bungalow was built for the commanding officer as the internal accommodation was considered hopelessly old-fashioned. The main water tank became the emergency fire-fighting supply.

Blacksmiths at work in the restored forge. Housed in the West Haxo casemate, next to the 7-inch RBL Armstrong gun, the forge was installed to serve the garrison early in the 20th century after the guns were removed. Demonstrations take place on certain event days.

The 60-pounder BL gun of 5-inch calibre was the medium gun of the Royal Artillery from early in the 20th century and saw service during both World Wars. A battery of Royal Garrison Artillery trained on these guns at Fort Nelson before the First World War.

Fort Nelson from the air in the spring of 1988. Five of the ten Second World War Anti-Aircraft ammunition stores (magazines) remain on the Parade. Two have been preserved, flanking the present Artillery Hall. The three white buildings temporarily housed the larger exhibits.

In January 1941 the Fort was bombed by enemy aircraft. The report in the Public Record Office for the night of 9/10 January commends the Fort for 'your unstinting efforts in supplying a further 1,220 rounds of ammunition by night to the various gun positions even though the Fort and its magazines were undergoing a heavy raid'. Fortunately the damage was not catastrophic, as it so easily could have been. But it is recorded that while the damage was repaired the Fort Nelson Anti-Aircraft battery was temporarily equipped with two mobile 3.7-inch guns like the one now on show in the Artillery Hall.

3.7-inch British Anti-Aircraft gun seen in a wartime photograph. This is a static mounting on which Britain's Anti-Aircraft defence largely relied. A mobile version was used in many theatres of war. The Fort Nelson Anti-Aircraft battery had static guns except for a brief period in 1941 when mobile guns had to be used due to enemy raids on the fixed position. Courtesy the Imperial War Museum

After the Second World War, Fort Nelson was used as a store by the Army and later by the Royal Navy. It became one of the many redundant but impressive relics of an obsolete military system. Neglected and insecure by the late 1970s, Fort Nelson was suffering from serious vandalism and seemed likely to be quietly reclaimed by nature.

GRAFFITI IN THE CELLS PASSAGE

Guard duty at Fort Nelson during the Second World War must have had its quieter moments. During some of these, soldiers made pencil drawings on the whitewashed walls in and near the Guardroom. Some of the sketches are quite elaborate. Here a soldier is shown firing a Bren gun at what appears to be Hitler's head. The small wartime garrison was supplied mainly by the Oxfordshire and Buckinghamshire Light Infantry (OBLI) referred to in the picture. Other graffiti contain useful notes such as the telephone numbers of Portsmouth Dockyard and the Hippodrome booking office.

The restored turret of the ammunition hoist and spiral stairs that connect with the main tunnel and served to distribute ammunition to the guns of Fort Nelson.

Fort Nelson
Before and after

Derelict and deserted, Fort Nelson might have gradually disappeared under the slow but relentless assault of nature. Rescued by Hampshire County Council, it would have remained a silent monument without a sympathetic use. The site was bought from the Ministry of Defence in 1979. Various ideas were explored for its future while clearance of rubbish and scrub growth and consolidation work took place. Commercial use did not appear feasible and as gradual restoration continued it was decided to open the Fort to the public in 1984. This would show the ratepayers what had been done so far and what might be achieved in the future. Specialist contractors, a Youth Training Scheme and dedicated volunteers from the Palmerston Forts Society based at the Fort, had already made good progress in what was to be over ten years work. Careful restoration and maintenance of a scheduled ancient monument of this magnitude remains a continuous process. Even in 1984 a few pieces of ordnance were shown, some being on loan from the Royal Armouries. The Royal Armouries at that time were considering ways of displaying some of the collections better outside the Tower of London and became interested in using Fort Nelson to house its artillery. In 1988 the Royal Armouries agreed to lease

Redan and west entrance before restoration, April 1980.

Many of the walls were covered in ivy before the restoration work. This was damaging the flint work.

Restored South-west corner of the Fort. The top of this wall was badly decayed. The flint work has reinforcement of brick piers (counterforts) linked by blind arches. These are intended to strengthen the large areas of flint that would be unstable otherwise and were never intended to be open.

The Royal Armouries' own self-propelled 25-pound gun in action on the parade at Fort Nelson. Its service history is unknown, but it has been painted in the colours of the 90th City of London Yeomanry (Royal Artillery), which landed in Normandy on D-Day, 6 June 1944. XIX.527

Fort Nelson from Hampshire County Council. The County would continue to restore the Fort at its expense while the cost of converting it into a museum would be borne by the Royal Armouries. The tremendous programme of restoration and conversion works culminated in the opening of the Fort as a fully established artillery museum and historic monument in 1995. Since then, the collection has continued to grow and interpretation has improved, bringing more and more visitors. Live interpretation, using both staff and volunteers, is a vital part of presentation at the Royal Armouries. As well as the museum galleries and re-creation of original armament, the use of selected pieces from the collection for firing and living history displays are a popular way of bringing the history of artillery and Fort Nelson to life. The Portsdown Artillery Volunteers, the uniformed section of the Palmerston Forts Society, represent the part-time Victorian soldiers that would have formed the garrison for the vast Portsmouth Fortress. On special days they demonstrate the working of the Fort's artillery. In addition you may see them firing the Victorian 16-pounder field gun, fully restored and with its limber; sometimes it is brought into action by horses. Or you may find them explaining the underground magazines or having a meal in the barrack room. Visiting enthusiasts demonstrate all forms of artillery, from the time before gun-powder was invented through to the mid 20th century. Mechanized transport transformed artillery mobility; special events show the Royal Armouries' own Sexton self-propelled gun on the move and enthusiasts bring their own vehicles to show guns, tractors and support vehicles in use.

Above: The 16-pounder RML field gun, introduced in 1872 was a heavier version of the Royal Horse Artillery's 9-pounder. After breech-loading guns were introduced for the regulars, obsolete 16-pounders were issued to Volunteer Artillery who had them into the early years of the last century. By then they were hopelessly out of date. A replica limber of this gun has been built to allow it to be demonstrated by the Portsdown Artillery Volunteers. XIX. 395

Below: A corner of the pleasant redan courtyard showing the architecture reflected in one of the panelled and glazed screens erected during the restoration and conversion of Fort Nelson. The bronze 13 inch mortar was cast by Jan and Pieter Verbruggen in 1779 at the Royal Brass Foundry, Woolwich. XIX.298

Glossary of Artillery

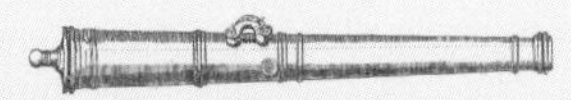

Artillery *Projectile* weapon too heavy to be carried and used by one person.

Armour-piercing Abbreviated as AP. A solid projectile often specially shaped and hardened or of special material such as tungsten steel to penetrate armoured vehicles or naval vessels

Bag charge *Propellant* charge for a gun contained in a cloth bag.

Base ring Projecting moulding at the widest point of the breech of a *smoothbore* gun.

Bed Support for a gun or mounting but more commonly for a *mortar.*

BL Breech-loading. Usually understood as a gun that loads at the *breech* and uses a *bag charge*. An example is the 5.5-inch BL *gun/howitzer*.

Bombard A large-calibre stone-throwing gun.

Bore The internal cylinder of a gun; also used in the sense of *calibre*.

Breech The rear end of a gun barrel. If breech-loading, *BL*, a mechanism that allows the gun to be loaded at the breech while ensuring gas-tightness or *obturation* when closed.

Button see *cascabel.*

Calibre The diameter of the inside of the barrel or *bore*.

Cannon Originally a heavy weapon of relatively short length. It has come to be a general name for any piece of smoothbore artillery but at Fort Nelson you will find gun used instead of cannon except where the gun is in fact a cannon.

Cascabel The rounded breech end of a muzzle-loading gun. It is finished off with a *button*.

Carriage Support for gun barrel and sometimes providing for its transport from place to place. It may also have a mechanism to control recoil. See *mounting*.

Carronade A short large-calibre weapon introduced by the Carron Company of Falkirk in 1779, the heaviest version was the 68-pounder of 8-inch calibre known as the 'Smasher'.

Curved Fire The path of a projectile fired at high angle by, e.g., a *howitzer*, useful when attacking protected positions or searching the reverse slopes of an obstacle.

Depression Negative angle made by the gun barrel in relation to the horizontal. Necessary for firing at targets lower than the gun position.

Driving band A ring, usually of soft metal, secured in an annular groove near the base of a projectile. On firing the band is forced into the *rifling* to spin the projectile and seal the propellant gases.

Elevation Positive angle made by the gun barrel in relation to the horizontal. Within limits, increasing elevation increases the range achieved by the projectile. Set by wedges, elevating screw or elevating quadrant and pinion.

Extractor A manual or more commonly an automatic device that removes the fired cartridge case from a *QF* gun.

Fin stabilized Abbreviated as FS. The earliest illustration of a gun, from 1326, shows it firing a heavy arrow with metal fins. This is a fin stabilized projectile. In modern gunnery it has been used in smooth bore tank armament to stabilise very thin dense *armour piercing* or AP projectiles in combination with a discarding sabot or DS. Such a projectile is known as APFSDS.

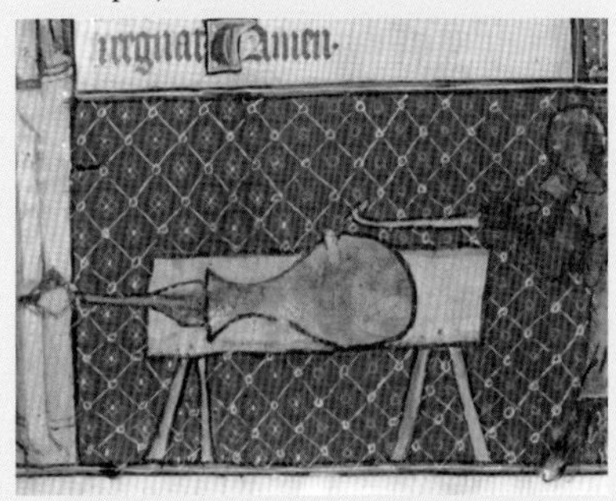

Fuse Usually spelled fuze in 19th-century British service. An ignition device for a *shell* that initiates the main charge at the desired moment.

Gas check A soft metal plate or ring attached to a projectile to prevent burning propellant gases form leaking past the projectile. Usually provides for rotating the projectile by engaging in the *rifling*.

Gun/howitzer An artillery piece that combines the role of both flat trajectory and *curved fire* weapons. They may be either *BL* or *QF*. An example of the latter is the British 25-pounder introduced in 1939. By pivoting the barrel at the breech end high angle fire was made possible. A wide variety of trajectories was provided by this and by arranging for a choice of charges to be loaded.

Howitzer A short-barrelled weapon designed to fire explosive shells usually at high angles of *elevation*.

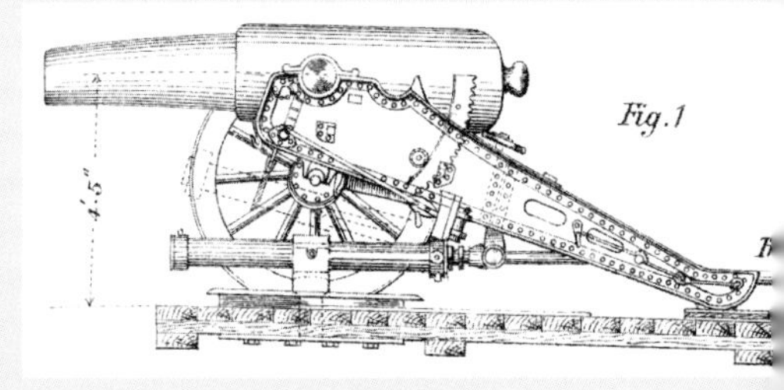

Limber Usually two wheeled device which, when linked to a two wheeled gun carriage enables it to be moved over a distance. Often arranged to contain stowage for ammunition and small stores.

Linstock A device for holding a length of *slow match* with which to ignite the priming of a gun.

Match, slow Hempen cord treated with saltpetre to ensure steady burning.

Mounting A support for a gun, a term mainly used to refer to those in naval and fortification service.

Mortar A short-barrelled weapon firing at high angles of *elevation*.

Muzzle The open end of a gun barrel from which the discharged projectile emerges.

Muzzle ring A moulding or swelling at the *muzzle* of a gun barrel.

Obturation The means of preventing gas escape at the breech of breech-loading ordnance.

Projectile Solid object, e.g., a *shell,* that comes out of the muzzle of a gun.

Propellant An explosive or fast-burning substance such as gunpowder or cordite used in a gun to propel the *projectile.*

QF Quick-firing. A breech-loading gun that is loaded with ammunition in a metal, usually brass, cartridge case containing its own means of ignition. (Sometimes mistakenly called a *shell-case.*) Often the projectile is attached to the cartridge to form 'fixed ammunition'. The British 18-pounder QF gun is a good example of a gun using fixed ammunition. A true QF gun has a mechanism for controlling recoil and returning the gun to the firing position. This is known as recuperation and run-out.

Quoin A wedge used to support the breech of a gun barrel at the desired angle of elevation.

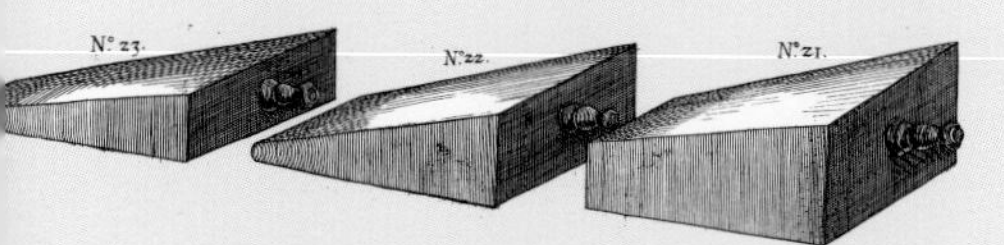

Ramrod A tool used to push ammunition into the barrel of a gun.

Recoil The equal and opposite force generated when firing a projectile. Various means have been adopted to resist or control this potentially damaging force. One of the most impressive was the Moncrieff mounting.

Rifling Spiral grooves machined into the bore of a gun to impart spin to the projectile. Spin is necessary when firing pointed elongated *projectiles* to ensure that they fly point first.

RBL A Rifled Breech-Loading gun, but usually restricted to describe the British guns built to Armstrong's system.

RML A Rifled Muzzle-Loading gun, also referred to sometimes as a muzzle-loading rifle.

Shrapnel A shell containing musket balls or small pieces of metal intended to be fired against troops or aircraft. A small explosive filling is provided to burst the shell and throw the contents forward when desired. This is arranged by setting a time fuze. Named after the artillery officer Henry Shrapnel (1761–1842) in 1852 although he had come up with the idea in 1784.

Shell A projectile that is hollow in order to contain a filling, for example high explosive (HE). Alternative payloads include propaganda, smoke, nuclear, biological or chemical substances.

Shot A projectile that is solid. Early shot was spherical and was usually made of stone or cast iron. Known sometimes as 'cannonball'. Later, special shot could be *armour-piercing* (AP) for example.

Smoothbore A gun whose bore is machined smooth, i.e., has no *rifling.*

Sponge A tool consisting of a wooden rod fitted with a sheepskin or lambswool head for cleaning the bore of a gun.

Trail The body and rear of a gun carriage that supports the barrel and transmits both the weight of the gun and the force of recoil to the ground.

Traverse To move a gun through an angle in the horizontal plane to aim it or 'lay for line'; usually 'training' is the term used on board ship. In fortification it is an earth bank protecting or separating buildings.

Truck A small wheel on a gun carriage. Often made of solid wood for naval service, for garrison service trucks were usually cast iron.

Trunnion A cylindrical or slightly tapered projection on each side of a gun barrel to allow the barrel to fit onto the carriage and pivot in the vertical plane in order to elevate and depress.

Turret A rotating armoured housing for one or more guns, usually fitted to a warship but sometimes found on land for coast defence.

Wadhook See *worm.*

Wad, Wadding Some elastic material loaded between projectile and propellant and in front of the projectile.

Worm A tool consisting of a wooden rod fitted with a helical metal end for extracting debris from muzzle-loading guns.

Parts of a Gun

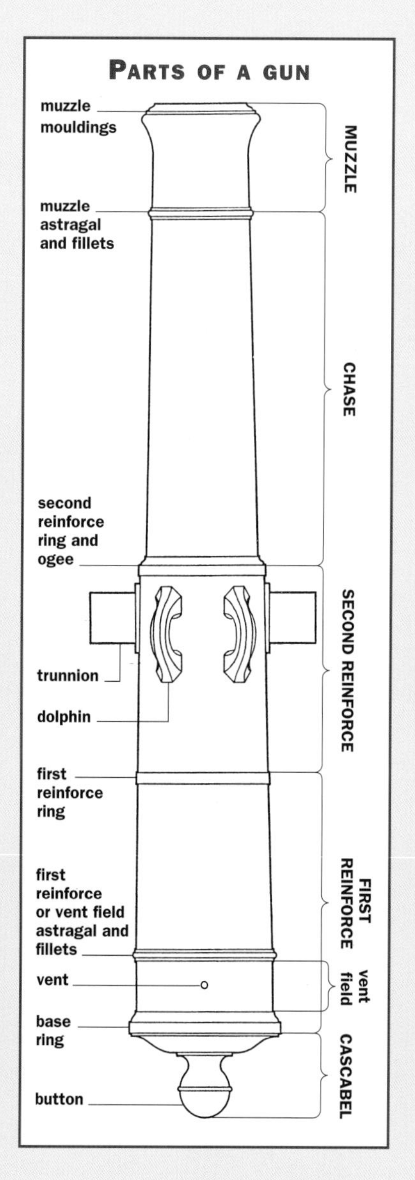

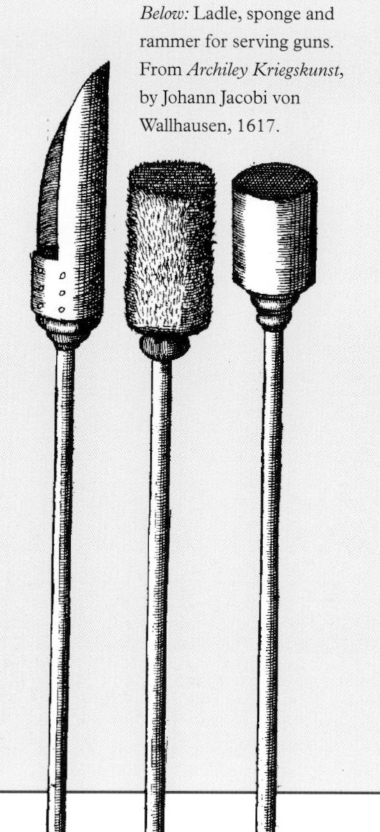

Below: Ladle, sponge and rammer for serving guns. From *Archiley Kriegskunst,* by Johann Jacobi von Wallhausen, 1617.

The White Tower, the oldest part of the Tower of London, built about 1078–1100.

Right: The recently reconstructed Line of Kings display.

Below right: Armour of Henry VIII, made in the royal workshops at Greenwich, 1540. II.8

THE TOWER OF LONDON

The Royal Armouries has occupied buildings within the Tower of London for making and storing arms and armour for as long as the Tower itself has been in existence and for display purposes since at least the 15th century.

With the establishment of its other two museums in Leeds and Fort Nelson the Royal Armouries in the Tower now concentrates upon the display and interpretation of its historic Tower collections, its own long history in the Tower and the history of the Tower itself.

The public displays of the Royal Armouries in the Tower of London are now all housed in the recently renovated White Tower in a series of themed galleries, each telling one aspect of the long story of the development of the great fortress and its armoury.

- The Medieval gallery traces the development of the castle up to the 16th century.
- The Royal Armour gallery contains the best collection of royal armours in Britain.
- The Ordnance gallery tells the story of the Board of Ordnance, which supplied weapons to the British armed forces around the world from the 15th century until 1855.
- The Small Armoury recreates the mass displays of military weapons and equipment which decorated the Grand Storehouse.
- The Spanish Armoury recreates a propaganda display first established in the 17th century which purported to show weapons and instruments of torture taken from the Spanish armada of 1588; most of them in fact were taken from Henry VIII's arsenal in the Tower.
- The Line of Kings is an interpretation of the greatest of the Tower's propaganda displays of mounted royal armours.
- The Artillery Room displays cannon used or captured by British forces as they were displayed in the Grand Storehouse and tells the story of the fire which destroyed it in 1841.

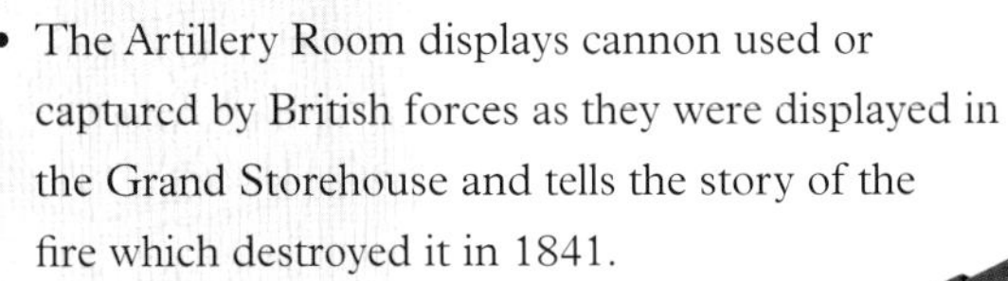

- The Victorian Tower gallery contains several 19th-century models illustrating how the castle was changed and restored in the 19th century as it ceased to be a working arsenal.
- There is also a temporary exhibition gallery which houses a succession of Royal Armouries exhibitions.

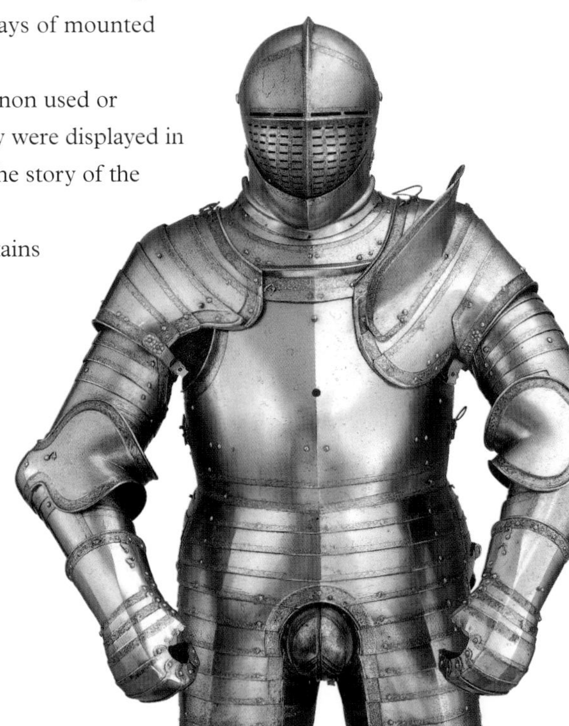

The Royal Armouries Museum, Leeds, viewed from the River Aire.

The Royal Armouries in Leeds

The Royal Armouries Museum in Leeds was opened by HM The Queen on 15 March 1996. Designed as a museum for the 21st century, it is the new home for the national collection of arms and armour. It uses up-to-the-minute techniques to interpret its world-class collections: live interpretations take place daily, and there are computer interactives and films in every gallery. The Newsroom acts as a venue for the interpretation of Contemporary Issues and there are practical workshops in the Craft Court where working armourers, a leather-worker and gunmakers can be seen. Outside, live demonstrations of skill at arms, jousting, falconry and hunting dogs take place and the animals trained for this can be seen in the Menagerie. Temporary exhibitions take place regularly. The principal galleries are themed to explain five key aspects of the collection:

- The War gallery traces the story of personal arms and armour on the battlefield from antiquity to the present day.
- The Tournament gallery charts the development of the major types of tournament. Displays include two of the armours made for King Henry VIII.
- The Oriental gallery concentrates on the great civilizations of Asia divided geographically into zones covering central Asia, Islam, the Indian subcontinent, China, Japan and South-East Asia.
- The Hunting gallery illustrates the story of hunting by topics such as hunting with crossbows, bird hunting, big- and small-game hunting, whaling, hunting in India, hunting swords, exquisite hunting weapons of the 17th and 18th century, airguns, target shooting and clay-pigeon shooting.
- The Self-defence gallery deals with the use of arms and armour in civilian life, charting the attempts by governments to control the ownership and use of weapons. The gallery also deals with the history of the arming of the police and other official organizations.

The elephant armour, Mughal, about 1600.
XXVIA.102

Display of armour from the 15th to the 17th century in the War gallery in Leeds.

Above: A member of the Brockhurst Artillery First World War re-enactment society shows a young visitor the purpose of the No 7 dial sight on the 18 pounder QF gun at one of the frequent event days.

Right: Firing in progress at one of the big 'Artillery through the Ages' event days at Fort Nelson.

Fort Nelson

Two visitor attractions in one

Fort Nelson was opened by the Duke of Wellington on 1 April 1995. This large site houses the Royal Armouries world-class collection of artillery. It contains a combination of traditional high quality galleries set in imposing architecture and modern interpretative techniques. Video presentations, hand-held audio tours and optional guided tours with a friendly and knowledge-able guide – all help give a better understanding of artillery and fortification. Another very effective and popular method of revealing the human stories from the past is provided by costumed interpreters. Fort Nelson has become well known for the varied events programme that helps bring the Fort back to life not only with the Victorian volunteers but for other periods right back to the Romans and on to the 1950s. There is a tremendous following for our open air Summer Band Concert in the spacious arena of the Parade surrounded by the ramparts, ideal for viewing and with space to set up picnic tables.

Fort Nelson is a great educational resource both for the collection and the building. Support and information for teachers planning schools visits is available and special programmes can be provided.

The Fort has attractive facilities for a variety of private and business functions. It is popular as an unusual venue for civil weddings – complete with a celebratory gun salute if required. The Officers' Mess and adjoining rooms are also popular with companies running training courses away from the distractions of the office. There is also a choice of fine surroundings for anything from a cocktail reception, to a buffet supper or formal dinner.

Above: Restored from a derelict state, the Officers' Mess and other elegant rooms on the upper floor of the Redan can be hired for a wide range of private and business functions.

Right: Note-taking during a visit. This Russian gun was taken by the British and French allies during the Crimean War.

Catering is provided in-house for the Powder Keg Café with adjoining Palmerston Room. For special functions nominated high quality outside caterers may be brought in by arrangement with the Events Manager.

For more information about the Royal Armouries visit our website at **www.armouries.org.uk**

Designed by Royal Armouries Design
Royal Armouries Museum,
Armouries Drive, Leeds LS10 1LT

First published 2000, reprinted 2002, reprinted 2004

ISBN 0 948092 40 8
Printed in Great Britain